The
Chicago
Poems

The Chicago Poems

CurtisTaylor

Geo-Frame Publishing Company

Copyright © 2006 by Curtis Taylor. All rights reserved.

Printed in the United States of America.
ISBN: 0-615-13216-2

This book is dedicated to
Georgina Susan

Introductory Word

I hope these poems help make moments for the reader. Chicago, for me, is less a Stacker of Wheat or Hog Butcher and more a young woman, or young man—beautiful, stylish, and narcissistic (have you seen The Bean?). I hope these shared moments affirm this city.

—Curtis Taylor

Acknowledgements

I would like to thank my wife, Georgina, for her years of friendship in support of my writing. I would also like to thank my talented sons, Nathan and Philip, for their support and appreciation of my artistic talents. And special thanks to Nathan for the Chicago skyline illustrations.

I could not publish these works without mention of my parents, Mary and Donald Taylor and others who have encouraged or taught me over the years including Richard Ketchum, Richard Wietfeldt, and Mark Rosenberg.

I must also thank certain artists with whom I have grown and who have encouraged me along the way. This would include Bonnie DesChamps and Francois Briere, the fine jazz duo from Quebec City; Ernie Mansfield, one of the world's great flutists and composers; and Katie Ketchum—super songwriter, singer, teacher and playwright. All artist-friends for many years.

Last, but in no way least, I happily thank Anita Haran, a fellow Chicagoan, who has also encouraged my artistic efforts for many years. In addition I would like to thank the Chicago Historical Society for their permission to use the archival photos used in this book: Hydrant Days, page 10; Newsboy, page 14; and Kids on Corner, page 28.

Table of Contents

The Merchandise Mart 1

Sunday Afternoon at the Art Institute 3/7/93 3

Of Small Cold Lungs 4

The Garbage People 5

Alexander Ice Cream Trucks 6

The Billboards from Van Buren Street On 7

Gouster 8

On Learning the Sacraments and Color 9

Hydrant Days 11

Lake Michigan Beaches 12

Cars-Off-a-Truck-in-the-Middle-of-the-Street-Man 13

There, But for the Grace of the Chicago Sun-Times 15

Reconciliation 16

Chicago's Ceiling 17

Old Town 18

Trotter's Kitchen 19

C.T.A. Bus Ride 21

Limousine People 22

Where the Mob Used to Live 23

Because the Gods Had Gone To Market 24

Chicago, Young Woman 25

Of All the Many Reasons Children Don't Live in Cities 27

On the Corner, Always Near Some Corner 29

To Another Teacher in a Faculty Lounge 30

Worms That Churn 31

A Room for Music in Mrs. Griffin's Funeral Home On
South King Drive 32

The Crossing Guards 33

The Chicago Hot Dog 34

Chicago Winter Morning..35

Jazz Sonnet 36

Last Days of My Jazz Dad 37

Soybeans and Peashooters 38

On Midwest Evenings in Cranking Days 39

Walking to Work in Late May 40

The Murder of Mrs. White 41

Christmas Eve in Hyde Park 42

The Color of Gray in Chicago's Ceiling 43

Nothing Pumps and Touching Is Cold 44

Her Backyard Is a Tall Red Haven, Roses, Gladiolas 45

On an Abandoned Four Cylinder Motor...............................46

Parking Lots at Governors State University 47

The Chicago Window 48

Dear Teacher of Geography in Chicago Schools 49

Flying Into Town 50

Pig Ear Sandwich Truck... 51

Basketball Boys at Dunbar High School 53

The Merchandise Mart

This oracle of coins
From cigarette booth to cab stand—
Swallowing sky,
Embracing a river's back-flows—
Its hushed voice
Moving with nylon legs
And a timbre of brushed trench coats,
Silk ties, swinging in clicks of heels.

Affronted gods of this town are busted and bronze.
Cool and hard they keep watch
On a city with hard edges.

This motion is worth a word or two.

Protecting Orion's walk
And warehouses, grim facade—
Remaining a bully in its neighborhood
With wizened big shoulders it sits
Listening smugly to pilgrims
From glass and chrome tribes
That tap brass coffers
And dance in jostling herds,
Transporting its unbent ear
With talent-laden ice and drifts
Under a supplicating western skyline glow.

Sunday Afternoon at the Art Institute   3/7/93

In our billion dollar island
In perspective like Jatte, struck
With technique or galloping to our next canvas horse
We move on Sunday with Seurat, Monet, Holder,
Picasso plucking and concerned with lessons and bent
We sit and let the dog play,—not a scratch is made—
We study and nothing moves but the Siene,
Not shade or air or the layered walls of our enclosed valve.
We shuttle or some other dance
Too quickly to see our painting, let alone 1,000.
We have no time to meet an artist, so we simply become one—
In our billion dollar island, staring down a Sunday
Afternoon on Grande Jatte you mock us, or
We become your silly mirror, not recognizing ourselves.
Dabbing in composition we move little,
So like that man with a long pipe, lounge-staring
Into nowhere, away from the painting we dance
In VanGogh's bed, blinded by Matisse's blinds.
Many visited act out their money's worth,
It's difficult to know,—smell things in a crowd, so
Monet's waves went into skys, Picasso was over-framed,
Guilty with centuries we numbered our tenderness so
In perspective, like Grande Jatte, struck with technique
We danced strangely before paintings.

Of Small Cold Lungs

In winter's bite
I wail in stilled blood,
at my ear's numb, flapping tune
tune,
juices in my head still
still swimming in early dream,
I wait while my eyes pop
tears at sluggish morning light.

Pole and I stand studious,
dumb and black and empty,
waiting in a thin coat,
dry-icing in a hall along a city.

Rigidly my only friend
galvanized and frost bitten,
reminds my blistered face
some black child's toes fell off—
that blankets are short
under a bitter hawk,
and crystal drifts
won't churn cheese
in an empty milk and dry powdered morning
where mother breakfast should be—doors
bang long into the gnarled air
of small cold lungs
tucked in with morning story.

The Garbage People

Three of them swagger-walk
Around their lunch, around their baby blue truck.
Big-bellied boys and girls with big faces, smiling
As clean as wrapped candy
In jean jackets, long gloves, boots
They swing to all directions
Banging out prayers on fifty-five-gallon drums
And raising their arms to God's mess.

Humor is hard in their eyes,
Eyes that erase and carefully blink
Through sweet smells over wasted days,
Into ears that listen to oozes from gold cups
And crackling drinks in foggy plastic—
They dutifully pick up fishes and loaves
Tilting at Baal's moving altar.

They are the Other people, reversing in high pitch,
Living in our childhood gangway in Other streets
From Other maps, keeping safe
In anOther place.

They possess bright houses and teeth,
Purchase time with their hands,
Cleaning space between bloods and mixing
An evolution of animals from chards in a drum.

Alexander Ice Cream Trucks

An island of ice and broken motors
Stinging hot drones in old circuits and scratchy tunes
In a mono-grooved song and radio torture
In a rush and rust of five-color decals plastered
Down a packed street, bumps an ice cream man.

His popsicle heart pumps with ice-watered blood

Out to pullulating hands

In shades of airless shadows,

From a visored window flows cream and sticks

To a dinner group following placement etiquette,

Politely yielding to strangers

Bouncing dangerous babies near curbs

Sitting neatly on fenders and burning bumpers

While Alexander's wide windshield eyes stare

Down the street of avenue hands.

A counter dance shuffles on dirty metal
Near the rebuilt sounds of muffled fun
Opening rubber rimmed doors like ventricles,
Or patting coins, circling parties and wishing pennies
Until the truck and its heart become a driven atom—
A red-lettered chariot, conquering pockets.

The Billboards from Van Buren Street On

I know every inch of these bars—

Every cracked vinyl stuffy-lumped stool,

Those warped cement corners where angular people

Miss cups while pouring low,

Wee at shadows on walls under billboards

Of giant swollen elegant ladies

Serving crystal whisky

On wet-look lips, then smile with

Athletic cocks and pelvises.

I've dealt with these saloon customers

As they roll and cuff each other,

Bleed thin blood, rend tears

From their children's flesh, weeping—

Then cussing and barking dog-bark cusses in white heat,

Then softly drift into shadowy lanes.

I know every inch of those paper thin women.

And those sotted men who miscarry themselves.

Gouster

Left over from his daddy's

shoes, turned up and pleated

wide, black, relaxed, big and

tough, the gouster walks to strut his stuff.

A dude to the nth, humbug

on a wintered night, pimped past

Picasso—indigo in individual.

He is the city felt-brim tilt—

long and lean from his neck

down to his tails and cashmere labels,

blowing and clapping in cold baby-man's breath

at a schooled doorway, lightly schooled.

Silently leaning, quietly in

wing-tips, his clothes are bright sparks

of expressive cuts in an infinite tapestry—

for the gouster—

a loose tie.

On Learning the Sacraments and Color
(From Dominican Nuns That Loved Our Children)

When color was on purpose

I learned color from woman hands—

Orange, orange in edible crayons

And yellow and white on suns, buses, and painted juice glasses,

Pure color ran purely from morning's moons—

How white Dominican white was along a nun's brow.

Starched and black with beads we lined up in rows—

Neither the colors nor women left instructions,

But red made me king of fears, I bled too little to forgive

Too much—to see, to see, to see a miracle or two—

Our eyes were more than blue or brown

And brown was the color of Carmelites

Or a visiting priest that had spoken with dying people.

Yet color was something to manage, hold up or drink

Out of temperas, or Kool-Aid, or paper in selectors on ringless fingers.

Color wound its stainless way around my senses

And lit my skin in deep genuflection—

Forgiven—I rested in my place in the dark,

Then I let the color blind me, through clouds,

In all the holes of my head.

Courtesy of Chicago Historical Society.

Hydrant Days

Hydrant days, when criminals win with wrenches
And God's flood from a pipe
Charges blue into a sky's white foam,
And cold jaws of children who rain down
Laughter from a sweated height like heaven bursting,
Their backs tied with skirts and shirts
And little hair on chests and small crosses
Bending and waving in a fender-tide,
Little sticks and gummy sludge
Sailing to new worlds,
Land on curbed islands, grinning pirates
Surfing cold ice tides, flooding Goodyear
In this fountain and spewing, then rises up
Some child with wet teeth laughing
Like a rabid dog, shivering and naked—
In our wordless shouting summer fount whose joy
Escapes from cut feet and this bully
Called July.

Lake Michigan Beaches

Lake Michigan beaches are made
of dead horses and sticky stuff,
They have a half-life in car carpets
And in baggy-kneed bathers that go color-flashing,
Or nourish in cans that cancer smoked gray
For dinner under an elm tree.

When sausage nearly burns all day heat
And crusts fly away in beaks,
Wriggling feet search a glistening grave
and castles smell of urine, as wet toes
Homestead a place where babies ruin
their hands with play and cola.

While on Oak Street children are sent away
and valleys run in pairs from breasts,
And flying youth crack thighs of bent joy,
so old men muster morning with benches
or pieces of chess and tables,
Then everyone rides the White Horse on flat bellies
near hot boxes—so goes Lake Michigan!

So go Lake Michigan beaches, so go tall toy sloops,
When tiny herds kick little ruts, skipping ancient stones
Along the sloppy walls of this undulating heart and tomb.

Cars-Off-a-Truck-in-the-Middle-of-the-Street-Man

This bent rushing, wind-configured fellow that slams cars down

In the middle of the street causes

Miles of motion in air-borne

Avenues that drip metal from truck racks,

Wrings porous sweat in sheets of flesh

Bumping a tidy road for carry-on

Trucks that a dealer's reflected

Windows are (for a while) his walled shirt

Of barrels and safety-island safety flying

Blink in the sun's white breast, twinkle and charge

Air traffic and an idea of work

With a vehicle in his rolling brow and eyes—

Moves deadly heavy and empty things in wrinkled tracks.

Courtesy of Chicago Historical Society.

There, But for the Grace of the Chicago Sun-Times

There, but for the grace of the Sun-Times, go I
Or all who've worked between cars
And you, old man
Paying dimes to a young man—
Both of you racked with cold, black and old—
Silent and moving under a bright blue roof of winter,
Whispering through your whiskers and leathern face,
While the boy, gangling in green limbs
Searches for hands, nods, or faces that will pay
You, old man, his street teacher—
Searching for a coin, an award like Oscar—only flat and dull,
A presentation that will buy immortality,
A pulpy ink mass, markers, some change and instant fame,
Each of you reaching toward each other's hands—
Dancing along salt-chalky King Drive
On a safety island, that little laughing altar
Of avenue and ceremony.
Ice and winds pull drops from your eyes,
My car brushes more wind through you
As sheet metal rumbling in traffic
Monoxides your business—
Drowns you—
But for the grace of the Chicago Sun-Times.

Reconciliation
(A Confession of a Chicagoan)

I was born in a central city

In a central part of a central neighborhood

In a central region of a central nation

On a central planet

In a central solar system

On a central day

In a central month

In the center of the century

During the center of night.

Yet—still—I leaned—

This way and that.

Chicago's Ceiling

Certain days cities have a ceiling on them,
walls—
and distances between all points
and the points are gray and busyness, soft,
and slow go
easy walking streets,
fruits in waking sounds
ripening to gray-domed clouds in a branching sky
of towns that have a ceiling on them—
closed store—
gigantic teepee—
tender morning and histories
of ears and peopled buses
turning through tendertime—
supple fall—
flat black fall afternoons;
city sound sends my
motions smooth—
motions taking me nowhere,
just settled in a moment
under ways of a city ceiling
one fall
one day.

Old Town
(1966)

Bohemian commercial

bright sunlit night,

brownstone sidewalk

carpet

picks and carries

merging rushing

passersby,

tight or slobberly

cool knit or loose strung

brand new or worn shiny,—sleek,

white on white or white on white,

or acne stitches on alabaster

pale blue pressed on corduroy, or

lowstrung navals on dusty bellies, or

blonde that sings on, or

devil-dipped hair-dos on

plug nickel whores at red blue taverns.

This is the night that presses against itself.

Trotter's Kitchen
(Dance of the Chefs)

Stuck in the wind of this onion city, these dancing stems,
These chefs, trimmed of their bitter, these hands and gifts
Along a stainless French oven whose talents
Of curved brass handles, strained sauces, bent chefs
And shifting in soft starch, faces rolling
Under table-numbered orders at Armitage,
A patterned dance checkered eyes to eye
Then quietly whipped in stainless clanks to bing and clang
With dish tympans or knocked chopping boards, drop and lean
Like prepped kale through red stems
In lemon and ice on these legs of food,
In a leaf whose heart and purple crown
Rose and ate with chakras and greens of a red brick floor,
Where musselled soup and lips on the skin of corn
So they did shuffle at the sauce station or the Grande,
Over slow-baked tomatoes whose meat and lust
Dove in hard frames of a clinging night.

In a stainless steel back-up of a forest floor
Cast up like wreaths in a Bacchus crowd,
Dill and watercress lost in fingered spoons—
As Chagall shook in a basil puree, a Matisse drapery
And all through these driven chefs, a breath and form
Of bones and glass, oil humming in tubes,
Spangling frost on voices and cream—
And all in a click of a night's gone dish and dance.

This shut and limbo at a stainless door
As black-suited Barcelona waiters shop for pastries
And joy took art in a child flying—
On plates and days of mugs and little pitchers,
Brimmed with—what was it? Corn soup? Beurre?
Or as they jingle linen under swift silver
Tied to Chicago in gone bubbling pots
With rosemary floating in saffron swordfish
Blue garlic and a float of oil-struck duck
And racks of lamb tilting at a grill
And spoons of hot and fired fire
In a white whose heat and brow and face
Tapped in gentle, even slices, paired and coined
With quail along its small bone.
(These meat grillers were the finest dancers struck by fire.)

All the slow mad dancing of twenty white-frocked angels
Like martial arts in a gentleman's degree flowed
In a pit of music swelled in a minute of war—
White currants in aspic of lilac cut with fingers and rings
Downed to these downing legs in sweet movement
Below a sweated spine or Bali secret,
Twirled in a Dervish, then soaked and mashed
Blading a knife and flint in its arch
This wrist or elbow in times of tongues and color.

How in rapture did this dance plan fold,
Tureened and layered in a shadowed world,
An unwrapped dream—hot, hot—dream dance?
Where does passion show its lumbar curve?
In this buzzing corpuscle, kitchen, or cell
On a morning past ether and sad songs,
While Boz Scaggs, Michel Legrand, and Eldridge swooned
Past a polyphony of rubber-lipped coolers, walls, and glass,
A plate was offered like a crisp flower spilling up
Toward a table and cuffs—
Then—
Breakdown began to take its wrap
And all cost was swept in a mop stick,
Rinsed when it counts—then stilled—in a general sense—
Of order. Then a bow or two was taken—
And the dancers limped in their bow,—
Then sleep,—and quiet of a still monster.

C.T.A. Bus Ride

Expiring hydaulic doors
Open to steps of a C.T.A. bus—

When an African-masked father-driver drives a green cab,
A history of choppy bolts becomes a smooth extrusion
Along sidewalks or lump prairie lots,—
When wheezing valve seats of silent cars
Din a low drum over asphalt's gray universe,
Chiffon babushkas and preened parochial boys
Jump to seats,
And the boys shout immortal taunts to girls,
While rattling clatter along stainless tubes
Whose handles to work accompany those spinning corners
Near poles to circular stages through a window—

Attentive ears of lined shops listening
To grinding gears near cemetery lawns
Passing between curbed lights, turning a turning bus
And a narrowing horizon.

Edging on a doctor's razor sharp cord,
Seesawing rubber floorboards over bangs
On rough stone of old avenues then
Knocking to a stop with a wheeze and a sniff—
Doors open and our barreling bodies exuent gently
From a clapboard cervix.

Limousine People

Down from Glencoe (its battles) over Sheridan (his battles)
Road to Lakeshore Drive, or in from Oakbrook or Flossmoor
Hovering just above tacky concrete
Then resting at the base of our largest throne,
Wide doors filled flush with chiffon and silk open
On long black cars swinging toward the Lyric Opera House—
Emptying caverns where sunlight bags
Behind tall columns and chimera chrome-stiff
Black and white like flowing chess
In tapered red-green colors on jewelled bosoms.

Or—delivering vita in pin-striped briefcases
From a synthetic womb birthing in tufted splendor
To our blasted rookeries with blank-gray and gritted stone,
Our city canyons under iron clocks of LaSalle Street, go bagmen,
Go limousine suit-men in tidy pleats.

Or—up in City Hall's temple
To tops of lined cars—
In private dens and dining rooms
From lawyer's suites in double-parked courts,
On walls of grid in wide-turning metal,
Letting in soft-cheeked registrars who,
Deep in dark glasses sit behind tinted windows
Turning wheels that crush some fruits of nirvana.

Down to song,
Delivering money,
Or—letting in muscle,
These limousines carry those limousine people.

Where the Mob Used to Live

Along Drexel, Randolph, or Longwood Drive
Where new signal gangs meet,
Where drivers used to meet in basements
Or on cement banisters, blasted grit porches
Along riverside or Cicero to Alexander Hotel rooms,
The Metropole near mirrors and small machine gun balconies
Peering from the corner bay window buildings
Off a river that had lost its sense
Running backward, still and deep.

Plumbing hallways underground,
Toasting hitmen that bought suits at Nash's—
Alphonso's dark heads drove
Into and out of Roosevelt's speakeasies
Along a tide to Michigan City in a storm of fedoras and Fords
Whose shadowy drinks smiled in Berwyn
In cheese-cutter hats and cashmere coats,
Slipped from numbers bags to buy molls at a moll house,
Developing a linen and velvet market in Kankakee
On tiled floors of fleshy crops,
Or striding along curved driveways
Pious churchmen whose politician hands
Preyed down Edwardian balustrades,
All in a din of a dream of a whim
Where the mob used to live.

Each brick, now a disintegrating hulk,
Each wall like a diseased lung, failing,
Each rotted frame heaving
Among quiet trees in breezy signs
Of old brew and silent revenge
Where the mob used live.

From the Turf Club to the Chez Paree,
In mass transit, like maggots,
This little world of tuna fish
Swam in the melt of their ice cream dish,
And spilled into penthouse realms
Into the sky and under the grid,
Into unfelt orgasms where gangs hang out, or
Where the mob used to live.

Because the Gods Had Gone to Market (Somewhere Near LaSalle Street)

When stores were opening and doors slammed shut,

A child began to fall, under night through a morning,

Mirrored in a brass plate with customer bells, falling,

Clanging to pavement,

Under rings and beeps of its National Cash Register,

In a pool of green and yellow blood

Where silver digs a grave in the middle of a trader's floor,

And gently rolled into heaven—

Under doors and brass and silver and reeling ticker tape

Because the gods had gone to market.

Chicago, Young Woman

Chicago, young woman with
    sloping shoulders wet and warm
    in a spring rain running
    spaghetti straps falling, in basic black—pumps.

Chicago, mirrors of torsos smiling
    along first and second stories,
    misting hard on a hard lake
    becoming a whisp on a breaker's edge—

Chant you now on a bus, Chicago
    corrupted with graffiti swirls
    neat and dressed in pulsing machines
    and gear boxes of priestly drivers.

This is your dance and run, kicking out images
Whose barely heard undersong:
(Red brick Spanish row houses
White sills, curved or straight
Backs of blackened stockyard brick,
A broken window just about everywhere
In certain areas lumpy
Avenues bunched with tracks of trains—
Magical gray that is brown
Or is it brown that's gray or concrete?)
Hear the hum of high-rise brothers aflame
And lit along Dan Ryan's dirty tracks,
Or jumping downtown in a cold dance
Near Irish stock market coffee houses,
Then settling in New Town rehabbed antique pads,
Then to Old Town jazz bands on pick-up Friday—
All this time you've embraced Sangamon Trials
    (tubes of your center) in asphalt.

Buildings for birds in glass-caged plazas,
Chicago, sweet young woman, an unnatural city
    pentacosting raindrops
    or snowballs, or dry hot wind,
Squeezing your wretched Lake Michigan lover
With your muscular and sandy legs, your ovum architecture
Tin and flat world tubes,

Peaked houses in square blocks with small lawns
And bungalows, in ordered sacraments,
And a place for a sloppy house or two.

Painted brick or empty lots blown
With tar and enamel scribble,
This note written in your fisted scrawl
With its early morning second wind
You dig back-hole holes, carry Van der Rohe bags
With fresh water power from the arms of gulls,

Under the sounds of gulls—

In your crystal curios with pidgeons and brogues,
Lawyers cuffs on woolen athletes
And miniature parks filled
    with memories of burning crosses—
Lust walked hand in hand with a Rush
    Street couple during gray dawn—silence.

Chicago, your sloe-gin juice and pelvic fountain,
    syrupy in a birthing way, running bud raw.
Crouched under a dark umbrella
You tilt upwind to a bar where your lovers booze,
Escaping the grasp of machines
As endlessly as the click and path of your heel.

Of All the Many Reasons
Children Don't Live in Cities

Legs that toddle can't stride iron beams—

Arms that swing loosely can't pull triggers,

Paste billboards, slap mortar on bricks,

Or lift wheelbarrows or steer anything.

Fingers that suckle in mouths move little money,

Can't autograph lithographs, baseball cards, fondle fifths,

Or rip theater tickets.

Feet too soft to walk brush few deep carpets.

The same is true of pumps too small to pulse,

Or warm streets in flowing red

When unclosed craniums whose gentle cups

Spill along aisles behind locked church doors.

All reasons of many

That children don't live in cities.

Courtesy of Chicago Historical Society.

On the Corner, Always Near Some Corner

Each of us seen in a single child's face—
Tired, red-eyed, wet-rutted
With tears that make a flat river
Between clutched pillow and shadows
Where silence knocks a dear mother
And a father whispers how he's driven by fear.

On the corner, always near some corner,
A silhouette in singular children becomes
A high priest or sacrifice given to evening, vespers
    from a tired and worn encyclical of daily dogmas.
Blistered with work, children hands offering
    weak limbs, weak limbs offering and whistling away
    (caresses) in the wind, building away fear
    and kisses to the center of the sky—
Where song introduces itself like a congenial business person
    and civilization's tumbling company arrives,
    sits at the sofa next to you, or the child—
    then leans over in comfort—to listen.

To Another Teacher in a Faculty Lounge

You have your radio and I have the Holy Ghost.

You say good morning and I say hi and that is all—

We say no more.

But I have the Holy Spirit and within me I grow
    and escape—

Now you turn off the radio, pick up
    the paper and read about

Some other teacher who had the Holy Spirit—who
    upon losing it,—died.

You remain happy and trivial

As I fold my angelic wings

Then leave the room in my responsible art,

Leaving you with your newspaper, a cup of coffee,
    solitude—quiet.

Worms That Churn

This Thanatopsis in a city park

And how I become part of a future tribe

Should I be buried here and return to my city.

Under cannon of war? A peaceful bean?

In the dew of April writhing

Worms that churn and make comfortable my finest bed

Speak the season in a fleshy twist,

Perennially flower along soft green lawns,

On tops of layered asphalt,

On tops of yaps of ancient dogs

Or children's voices whose music is lost

In battles of memory's memory,

Along the edges of wheels,

Near a statue, or tree, or war-hammered metal.

A Room for Music in Mrs. Griffin's Funeral Home On South King Drive

They that gather in velvet dens, near
    draperies that hang on a singular tree—
    each rolling in syncopated good-byes
    past singing hinges on doors to almost all
    American wars, (how wealthy we grew during Viet Nam).

Each to its own making, families in soil,
    reminding guests in small rooms, in rooms their prisons made
    of brass and wood, lead and flesh—
    past spondaic celluloid—twisted in army fires,
    each torch resonating in a dirge of silent shadows—
    assuming a signature of dust.

The Crossing Guards

Orange breasted Chicago winter penguins

Fly to morning corners of curbs,

Chilling for school kids in sateen blue jackets

Capped and crowned with visor bills,

Phosphorescent and waving paws with striped legs.

Mostly queen penguins

Stopping stretching to protect a herd,

On a cold, cold island in a cold,

Cold continent, thumped by cars,

Turning in a turning world, wind-whipped

Hands outstretched through freezing breath and vapors

At the pole of the world, under a truck-rushed sky,

Geared, blessing their red eyes whose hearts

Spin on a spinning road

Then swim under a metal sea whose currents

Flow with their hands and hearts of arms,

While listening for gabs and colors of children.

The Chicago Hot Dog

Out along a steamed cantos, from a lyric,
Cantata, cantable, sweet in yellow—
Melodies without words for a mouth
Dripping for relish or tomatoes
And seeds of meat, mostly Kosher
At 3,000 stands as old as stories,
And a given onion in its white chop
Dazzled a garden and garden bunched
Gave quick messages like Mercury or Apollo
Clamoring under tongs and celery salt rain,
Then gently nestled in soft wax paper at
A game—was it the Sox? The Cubs? All in a dog.
Under a heat lamp—without ketchup
Usually,—this inhalation.
A formula for fat, the algebra includes
The scent and salt of fries and cola.
Both song and mathematics lost
In a sea where dreams map out a lust
For exploring the surface of our known universe.

Chicago Winter Morning

A fisted year is hidden in pockets of winter,

Green falling in white dust.

Falling. Asphalt and white dust kiss morning in a burning

Snow. Up from melted white trades

Metal walls of alley-backed dumpsters bong

The city. And the crunch of wheels

Whose tired rollings tug before hands

At tubes that tie cities,

Spend snow. Winter trade walks trade

Under a phoenixed year, the she-bird

Rises up from pavements and alleys,

Leaving the lovers' powdered and winter blankets

Hobbled in the white lap of a gone sky.

Jazz Sonnet

These two shadows cast in blue
Begin and end this day outriding,
In small notes of fast scales
Pitched in the drift of our swinging lost waltzes—
Pounded in temperament to triplets of solos.

We that could be cool, hip, and sitting-in listeners,
Read-in. Close to ourselves in this night's middle
Reading in quadrants to ourselves what
We could have been, were, and what we'll be—
Sharing polyphony and rambling riffs
With those that have gone before or during.

Then we simply end this song on one long note,
Listening to shadows that precede our day
Looking toward a shadow-after,
In 7ths and 9ths until cut from roots,
Despite drums and our large opera.

Last Days of My Jazz Dad

In his warm, dark, last days
After an infusion of trees
Lit by moons and a star or two,
Deep in a narrow, small house
On a narrow small hill,
While aloneness sudden in his chest
And bones, walked naked at his door.

He came to terms with great memory
And how love made a creek in his body—
Sitting on his doorstep
Watching marvels and bits of matter
He would never know well enough,
Some regrets hung in his skin and eyes.

There would be a last hour to all this—
There would be a stillness beyond this stillness—
So an arching of light, his big bands, Eldridge solos
And my mother's singing breathed in his ears.

Then came the days of walking canes, pills and fading,
Along with visits to the store and his children—
The birds fed him so he saved the food—
He stared at the gray noise, and heard the bumps and racks of cars.

He was leaving what he helped make,
Music and Grandeur were slowly taking him.

Soybeans and Peashooters
(Ages Ago in Unincorporated Homewood)

Out from the Osage groves as fields spread
In neat leafy rows when pods were stung and silky
And crackling in our small palms and five-cent straws,
I became a life-size toy,
A hide-and-seek self, blind and deaf
      to my best friend's adventure—
So I shot him.
I shot him with wind in a fit in a mouthful of saggy-skinned
      soybean bullets from brown bags.
In my robber-stolen neighborhood I merely
Killed a cop or two while streaming from my lumpy cheek,
Slobber-shot through plastic pipelines that jumped color
From an ammo-dump farm.
Shooting our veins with pellets of lecithin
Without breaking the skin, without blood,
Without eating the shot in our machine-gun heads,
Hungry and safe in a mystical war, moments of eastern
Armies—far away and dead—
Late summer, invisible soldiers.

On Midwest Evenings in Cranking Days

On a long ago porch, in the stillness of early dusk

Draped along this holy, holy mystical rood

A jazz-wise shifting scale of clouds

And steady horizon of chromatic days,

Distant, along dillweed banks and black-eyed susans

When long lines are purple in evening whisps,

Cirrus adventurers that sup the moon

Drink and sing with us as we bend

From work and tractor-red fields.

Walking to Work in Late May

Econ
o
my,
a word for small gardens,
wire fenced
dripping with morning—
on a day when the lower end
of clouds were wet in grass
and plants planted in planting rows
forested along Walnut or Union Streets
ruffled by hard hands in Blue Island
or any small industrial suburb where paychecks cash
and the twist of salary in weedy ditches
in purple and yellow iris schedules
or red and white, white-red peony bushes
along the edges of working lawns
whose clumps house pass-book people
in rounded banks and bugs,
a folding green then yellow hay
becomes a grace (some slant of silence
leans into the next second)
of minutes
burnt for manna.

The Murder of Mrs. White

I lost a customer today to competition

For her breast and hair, her fair

Slightly wizened face and gentle gait.

O lost her on a referral, a commission

Existing before I could bid the job, her work

For a Williamsburg home on Lothair Avenue.

She wanted lace, or was it linen weaves?

Along blue shuttered windows with bony fingers—

Whose light was it in her porcelain brow?

She left my store for TV and a light lunch,

Only natural foods would do—

Cut by a knife whose edge sliced gracefully.

I saw the same commercial on TV and almost bought,

Buying (as I do) into murder, or at least the News.

With her face and mine under a sheet, carried by officers,

All was given, on special, sold, as is.

Christmas Eve in Hyde Park

This is a day I remember as a jollyhill
On my belly's sweater,
When my two sons leave me alone a little more,
When we stand in shopping lines
Or walk an icy court along brick and frame,
With gifts in flapping wind and flying arms
We separate another year—
Slowly, like jam traffic from candied jars.

This is a day I remember before morning leaves its cold bed,
When I long to hug my other's arms, wife-red cheeks,
When I let my agape grow
And I smash through my flesh to arrive
At Santa's brass music field from a Ginsberg shelf,
And a Salvation Army jangling in aluminum and dusty books
And glassy boutiques that direct me with fingers of scented doors.

This is a day I remember we climb out of booths
Sweaty, gaseous, like exhausted pipes humming,
When stomachs ache in chocolate and gift-wrap
Or white secrets of a blistered winter kill our noses
And our shattering eyes cry windy tears,
And our day is December and our year is a banquet
In a calendar-spent restaurant for a place to park.

This is a day I remember Philip sings
And Nathan flys into our gray sky, both with wings,
Both in baggy elbows and flappy jackets,
Under their mother's rustling purple down, limbless diving,
Philip in saffron, Nathan in green, herding plastic bags,
Animals of holiday with friendly jaws,
We rounded our lips for marzipan and roses—
Struggling home with numb parcels and ears.

The Color of Gray in Chicago's Ceiling

The color of gray in Chicago's ceiling
     Permeates our drawn skin,
Towers like a benign god
     Over our gothic buckling shops—

In baroque stillness this giant mural
     Rests its mountain feet,
Playing mother and father
     Over our family of rolling bedlam.

Its breath drops down in winter flashes
     To bite the faces of hustling clerks,
Transporting a viscera with icy tongs
     In butcher's color with leaden weight—

The color of gray in Chicago's ceiling
     Appears like Hardy's heath, often,
A voice emerging from its closed eye
     Whispering without vertizon or horizon.

Nothing Pumps and Touching Is Cold

(Re: a marble atrium near north Michigan Ave.)

What is this distaste I have for marble?
Why am I sick of this stone?
That cool distance,
That opaque wall,
That hurting smoothness
That crushing lintel,
Without color, without sound—
What makes me cringe at its design?
Are these dead veins? Is it this heaving stillness?
This finality is too much for me.
A cynical sickness from headstone
To baptismal font where moisture dries, encrusts,
Nothing pumps and touching is cold.

Her Backyard Is a Tall Red Haven, Roses, Gladiolas

She lives in the luxury of her husband's grave,
Bent over all flowers and patio furniture, wrought iron,
Crowded by chards in a dusty alley
And glass-glittering grids of nearby parks.
Her backyard is a tall red haven, roses, gladiolas—
From machines that rolled around her city garden.

She was silent and didn't understand her immortality—
Her greatness was made by my scribble scrawling in our air, my pen,
As I saw her momentarily brush and bend in the sweat of a petal,
Speaking under her breath the broken language of another continent,
Disgruntled with jets, conversing with insects.

On an Abandoned Four Cylinder Motor

Under this fence that walls a lilac bush
Whose height and perfume narrows between
Garages and their rippling tides of dry paint—
In an alley where weeds curb concrete—
Lies an engine empty of pistons, lining,
Head, manifold, and sparkless mold.

It is my engine trapped by my city,
My habit of movement in stilled and burning rust,
As if a grid were sketched under lights
Where wires and stars lost in a tube
Leave fire in a carbon-rodded cavity.

Once in the hope of a four-wheeled frenzy,
When poles of a spinning blue ball
Dropped its color between sun and rain,
I saw this engine in its feeling press
And peel along a driven moment.

Now, moving with a finer metal, I am part of its bodyless car,
Unrubbered, unset, reverberating with stillness,

Then left—
Upturned.

Parking Lots at Governors State University

These squares change colors every day,
Kaleidoscope movement—
Charged symmetrically, anchored in concrete
Posts and lights bound in fingers of sculptors.

Asphalt fields under a soybean dome
And divided by osage wires, barn rot, cattails,
They are a single path, blue roofed,
Walking home for open seasons. True.

Sloped, curbed, bordered, Whitmanesque, lit,
    circled, embracing,
A place for lost keys, a key for lost places,
Bundled in our metal boxes we burn
First burns, in tumbling engines.

The Chicago Window

Urban suburban picture window

For all housewives once surrounded by cities,

In a metropolis of large wars

And panoramas of glass, a sky through windshields

For a home's womb where living is—

Many a mother's view above a flower box,

Watching neighbors roll with their cars,

Providing a large ledge for eggs and a risen Christ.

Figures approached and left in their non-reflecting eyes.

This was the civic square of our open house,

A gift of motion under an oracle of light, court—

A matrix for bits of moons—

Each as unlike each minute to the next—

A mathematician's palette,

Almost coloring by numbers.

Dear Teacher of Geography in Chicago Schools

Plastic covered paper covered vinyl maps, your soft hands

Of lines on hands that effleurage the planet, backhanding seas

Gently rising across boundaries bounded by elevations,

False elevations and a real one.

> (How did you know about
> this little war zone in my neighborhood?)

Your world is flat, except at the edges

Where you are gently warped—rounded with old buildings.

Your hand crosses, or is it wafts, so many

Empty spaces where people should be—

Your hands eradicate famine and disease, poverty and hunger—

> (except for me as I smell the cafeteria fill
> with the hope of hot dogs.)

You legitimize generations topographically. A sun at night.

Your clockwork maps bed down with this disciple

And instruct,

Your Student

Flying Into Town
(From My Jet Window View)

All patches of brown houses
Pitched in squares beyond cold vacuum,
Steeled wings as small as rivets
Flowing over cirrus lakes
And cool green calm of a foamy silent shore—

Over Michigan, over Lake Michigan
High in a sudden square coast with mists
Rising boxes, sky pegs,
Hooked buildings called Chicago lumped in a cubist print.

Swivelling on a turning shadow under my wing,
Under dry and death-felt steel, losing blue and landing
Onto grays of a dotted grid, O'Hare
Just before blue lights, wears a concrete roar.

While civilization and sins hide in small boxes,
These houses and rows of houses moved swiftly
In a flow under my wing, under my roar.

Pig Ear Sandwich Truck

A tall man with greasy hands

Swollen fingertips and steamy boxes

Parks a truck on Racine

Connected to a sunny morning.

Folding bread and white enamelled doors,

Sceptering incense of mustard and vinegar

About, like letting Jordan flow

Over the noses of unbelievers

And into the watery eyes of workers.

BBQ pots begin to bubble stainless steel—

Molten sauce drips from tongs—

Bloody afterbirth prepared for licking,

While his future is mortared in a wax paper box

His rent is paid with child-like dishes in boats and foil,

Soft and hot.

A breeze in warm May, processed and slow,

Moves with him in his squared cavern,

Setting up spicy walls,

Lining his brow with crystal beads—

Salting his bread.

Basketball Boys at Dunbar High School

Basketball boys at Dunbar

Shoot hoop

New York—Twenty One—

Break, bogard, and drive on bent legs.

Under thirty-story gutters,

Carbon-blown and boarded views,

Under these props for a great play—

They pass, bow, and strut their double pump.

Tin-banged backboards ring in dull timbre,

Squeaky-shoed boys turn in charged courts,

Project booms rip sun-white clouds—

And the girls take a shot or two, also.

Note About the Author

Curtis Taylor has been a worker-writer most of his life. He received a B.A. in English and an M.A. in Literature from Governors State University on the wings of a Talent Competition Award. His poems have been published in Canada and England as well as in the United States. They have appeared in magazines, journals, and newspapers. He has also published songs that have been performed and recorded by jazz artists and are available on compact disc. This is his first published collection of poems.